THE STOICS GUIDE

TO THE CARE AND FEEDING
OF HOMO SENTIENS

–OR–

THE ENCHIRIDION AND THE BOTH OF YOU

CLIFFORD T. SMYTH

Introduction:

Stoic philosophy gives us useful tools, wise words, and powerful paradigms with which to frame our existence—in the world, in society, and within the universe. We are usefully taught how to frame our fortunes, misfortunes, situations, and struggles for the best possible outcomes.

Stoicism helps us to tolerate both tragedies and triumphs with poise, peace, and grace. What is missing is guidance on how to treat our inner selves in the process of dealing with the complex world of modern humanity.

Where stoicism typically fails is in guidance for the pursuit of everyday ephemeral happiness. We can be well satisfied with our life as being "the best possible condition" and still find life hollow and devoid of joy. An acute lack of joy can be debilitating—even to the point of being unwilling to continue–despite our overall satisfaction with (or acceptance of) our state of being.

In this book, I strive to relevantly present the refined gems of the stoic ethos provided by The Enchiridion, interpreted and supplemented with pertinent accompanying guidance on the care and understanding of our outer and inner self.

The Human Condition

The duality of existence is part and parcel of the human condition, as experienced by people everywhere since the dawn of culture.

As part of our early enculturation, we are taught to "control ourselves". This very basic need to maintain high-level control over inner impulses, drives, and feelings betrays the struggles that we will face for our entire lives.

Language constructs like 'self-control' and 'self-discipline' put into plain view the inner conflicts that we face. There is a 'self' that needs to be controlled, and a 'Self' that is expected to take control. From an early age, we are admonished for acting impulsively, for erratic or purposeless movement, for outbursts of emotion, or any kind of 'anti-social' behavior. By the time we are 5 – 7 years of age, we are expected to be able to 'act' with a degree of decorum and 'appropriateness' most of the time.

These early childhood milestones of enculturation are only the beginning. As we grow towards and into adulthood, we are expected to fully mold and sometimes subjugate our inner selves towards the goal of being "productive" and respected members of society.

The inherent conflicts of existing as a human being, as well as a member of society, become ever more evident as our self-image and social expectations range ever farther from the natural human being that found themselves thrust into the world.

It is as if we are cognitive and rational beings, forced by the vagaries of fate to share the mind of a bright but needy and sometimes capricious host. Many will relate to the common occurrence of going for a drive or a walk, only to "wake up" at our destination, having been brought there by their host of their own accord. We were 'lost' in thought, but our host is often perfectly capable of walking, driving, and many other tasks with only sparse guidance on overall goals and destinations.

This host, with all of its wonderful qualities, strengths, and weaknesses, is often poorly suited to exist in the world of culture without an ever-vigilant guiding mind. Unguided or poorly guided hosts find themselves as victims, trapped in servitude or abuse, haunted by vice, at odds with society, and on the wrong side of the prison gates or worse.

While we must learn to be wise and judicious guides of our hosts, we must also learn to be kind and generous masters. All too often we are told what we must do, the feelings we must learn to overcome, and the weaknesses we must not give in to. Conspicuously missing is wise counsel on caring for our host, that bright, impulsive, tender creature that we all inhabit.

I have found that a deeply useful model for thinking about the guiding 'Self' and the guided 'self' is one of a master and beloved pet. Our inner human being is very much like a bright animal version of ourselves. We learn to both guide and be guided by the animals in our lives, respecting their intuitions and considering their needs even as we go about our plans.

We don't conflate the needs and feelings of a beloved animal with our own, yet we give them the consideration and benefit of the doubt as we observe their reactions to and interactions with the world we present to them. We take them out on walks, give them rewards, admonishments, and treats. We make it a point to reward them for a job well done or even just for their kind presence. We try to find ways to include them in our lives in ways that we will find rewarding, and we take joy and pride in their joy. Why should we treat our inner selves with less regard and presence of mind?

Our inner self, host, or "pet" can be a tireless assistant, your powerful ally, and your greatest friend. Mistreated, ignored, and abused, he can become your worst enemy, your nemesis, your assassin. There is some evidence that many suicides are attempted or completed without premeditation or even knowledge before the fact. A host that has tired of life is a treacherous carriage indeed.

Our hosts—essentially unchanged since we were just beginning to form complex societies—are often ill-equipped to navigate the maze of constraints, incentives, and traps present in the post-primitive world.

To succeed in this new environment, enculturation is required. This process subjugates the impulsive behaviors of the inner self to the more thought oriented being of culture, constructed of a complex memetic web of belief systems, paradigms, and systems knowledge. The resulting personality construct is better equipped to methodically analyze complex choice trees, weigh risk profiles, and plan strategically. Not only is this resultant being more capable of thriving in complex environments, but he is also capable of ambitions, hopes, and works that transcend the capabilities of the host in which he resides.

But where does she come from? How does this bright primate become two beings in one? Why does this not seem to happen in the case of feral children? Insofar as this model may be correct or at least predictive, I do not have a definitive answer— but I do offer a hypothesis that at least gives us a useful model and a convenient explanation.

I propose that part and parcel of the process of enculturation can be thought of as the development of an alternative viewport on the world. We tell our children stories, speak of things that must be imagined because they cannot be sensed. Mommy will be home soon, the dog is in the other room, your sister will be gone for a few days, but she will be back with grandma—for all of these things, understanding requires imagining the implied scenario, a separate and imaginary point of view coexisting within the immediate awareness and sensorium of the human mind.

Gradually, this point of view is expanded with more complex stories, lessons, and the understanding of complex social systems with hidden levers of influence. I think of this process as the methodical creation of an "imaginary friend" within the consciousness of the human child.

Gradually, we ask this imaginary point of view to take an increasing role in the actions of the young child. We begin to demand that they "control themselves," wait patiently, be still, and other activities that overrule the impulsive nature of the toddler. Each of these tasks implies a controlling entity and an entity that is to be controlled. The implication that they are fundamentally separate is so obvious as to be often overlooked.

By 7 years of age or so, we expect this "imaginary friend" to be more or less in charge, and it is only with this being that we converse when we talk to our child in most situations. Only in moments of embrace, comforting, or calming do we seek to reach out to the inner being in our child after this point. Through this process, the human-animal becomes the human being, a fully realized sentience capable of much more than the bright bipedal creature in which it was made could do, left to its own impulsive nature.

Despite this metamorphosis, however, the inner self persists. Its viewpoint on the world is filtered through the enculturated self. She has learned to rely utterly on her guide, but still may rebel, fail, or freeze if pushed beyond the limits of her trust.

This relationship that we have with our hosts is one that is rarely elucidated in literature or culture, but it is surely the most critical, life-altering relationship that any of us will ever have. A deeper understanding of this relationship of the Self, to the self, deserves more than cursory consideration.

The Enchiridion Revisited

1

We do control some circumstances in our lives, but often, we have only the illusion of control and are confounded when we discover the deception.

Only our opinions, thoughts, intentions, and actions are truly ours to control.

In contrast, our desires, aversions, and feelings fall within that which we are responsible for but can often only influence indirectly.

Though they come from within us, we don't fully control our emotions—they are not truly ours to control. Our base emotions belong to our innermost self, and while we can calm and comfort ourselves, or tell ourselves that we must endure, we often cannot (or should not) ultimately silence that inner voice.

When it is needed—or at any time at all, speak with calm assurance to your inner self. If they are agitated or disturbed, you can calm them, comfort them, and offer them hope. As with a child, they only know what they are told.

Those things which we do not control include our health, which may fail, our property, which may be lost, our reputations, which may be defamed, and the actions, thoughts, desires, or feelings of others which may often fail to meet our expectations.

Even so, we may be blessed with good health, we may be rich, or we may have great fame among people. We may be loved, have true friends and a beloved family.

In any or either case of fortune, good or bad, we must understand that these things are not ours. They may be pleasing, or distressing, but they do not truly belong to us, and their presence in our life is not ours to control.

The things in our control are free and unhindered by their very nature. That which we do not control is weak and unreliable, enslaves us, is limited in nature, or belongs to others.

If you suppose that things which are slavish by nature are also free, or that which belongs to others is your own, then your way will be obstructed. You will find frustration, disturbance, unrest, and you will probably blame others or the world itself for your difficulties.

When you accept that only those things that are your own to control are yours, and that which is not yours to control belongs to others, then no one can compel you or restrain you. You will find fault with no one or blame no one, and you will do nothing against your will.

If this seems to you a very bold claim, it is. Achievement of this is a matter of understanding your will according to this new understanding of what is ours to control, and what is of others.

Aspiring to such great ends, remember that you must not allow yourself to be drawn toward the attainment of lesser goals. Instead, you must entirely abandon some aspirations, and postpone others until you have achieved progress towards this new understanding.

If you desire happiness and freedom, but also thirst for power and wealth, you will not achieve either. Power and wealth arising from a thirst to control that which is not yours will take you far from peace and enslave you. In being needful of both, you will fail on all accounts: your desire for happiness will limit your success, and your greed will prevent you from freedom.

Strive, then, to be able to say to every trial, triumph, and circumstance, "You are but a facade, and not truly the thing you pretend to be." After denouncing that which confronts you, examine the circumstance by the rules you have learned. Discover whether the circumstance concerns the things which are truly yours to control, or those things which are not. If it concerns anything not truly within your control, whether it is a disaster or good fortune, be prepared to say that it is nothing to you at all. True failure or victory comes only from within.

Even when they do not come from within, you may celebrate your victories. They are merely good fortune and are not yours, but just as you might find joy in the good fortune of a friend, find joy in the good fortune of your self. Be careful, though, to understand that this does not belong to you, and that which you celebrate today may easily be lost tomorrow.

Be mindful to not take pride nor shame in a victory or defeat that is not yours, but you may rightfully be proud of your correct and natural reaction to this fortune, whether good or bad.

Remember that just as we choose to rejoice in good fortune or lament a tragedy of fate, we must also be prepared to ignore it, as it was never ours to bear in the first place.

2

Remember that pursuing a goal promises the attainment of that goal—and that avoiding a circumstance promises the avoidance of the object of your aversion.

If you should fail to obtain the object of your desire or fall into the circumstances you had wished to avoid, you will suffer disappointment or grief.

By confining your goals and aversions to those things that are truly yours to control, you will not fall into circumstances that you dread, nor will you be prevented from achieving the aims of your aspirations. Do not promise to your inner self things that are not yours to give.

Instead of desiring friendship, desire to be the kind of person to whom people flock readily. Instead of dreading sickness or ill health, avoid sloth, poor habits, and excess. Do not desire wealth or fear poverty; instead, endeavor to be the type of citizen to whom wealth flows easily. Strive to be a person who can suffer hardship with grace and honor, and you will not fear financial ruin.

Until you learn how to have correct and healthy goals, and to not desire that which you may some-day—but do not yet—control, limit your desires and aversions. Even things that are worthy of desire may be beyond your readiness to possess. Desire or avoid carefully, and only that which you may possess or avoid, and even these things lightly and with caution.

Even as you choose carefully what to desire or avoid, of these chosen things, dream freely. Imagine being the person that you wish to become, and even (with caution) how that might influence your circumstances. Believe that you will become, within yourself, the person manifesting those desired traits.

Belief is a prerequisite of achievement. You must convince your host that as surely as anything else within your control, this too will come to pass.

These dreams are not for you. Dreams are for your inner self. They need to see the destination to find their way. They may believe in things which have not yet happened, but they will not believe in that which has not been made real in their vision.

Dreaming, do not fall into the trap of dreams—to imagine that by thinking it, it is done. You must stop short of imagining specific rewards, and leave your host with anticipation and desire rather than imagined satisfaction.

Dreams, which are in your control, must not be conflated with circumstances, which are not. A dream should not be a desire, or a fantasy, but rather an image, a symbol for a destination which you already possess but have yet to manifest.

Remember that dreams, manifest as actions, are the maps to destiny.

3

When considering the things in life that delight you, are useful or are beloved, remind yourself of their basic and general nature. If you are fond of a cup, remember that you are fond of cups. Perhaps of green cups with handles, of which there are many. Then, when the cup falls and breaks, you will not be disturbed, for there are many green cups with handles.

If it is a unique and rare object, remember that there are many unique and rare objects. Its unique and rare composition being its fundamental character, it is common. Even with people, those most enduring yet fragile of creatures, remember that people are beloved, and not only your spouse or child. This will help you to be prepared for even the worst of circumstances that can befall a person.

Avoid emotional attachments to objects. You do not own material objects so much as they benefit from you as their steward. You must be sure that you receive enough from their presence that the burden of stewardship is warranted.

You cannot – and should not – prevent your host from developing emotional bonds to other people. Since the beginning of mammals as social creatures, to be banished, isolated, or unloved was death. The vessel of your existence, your beloved host, is still very much that same creature. As a good steward, you should encourage them to make loving emotional bonds with worthy individuals.

This may seem antithetical to the stoic ethos, but it is not. Stoicism teaches us only to not consider such attachments as ours. To understand that they are valuable, as anything of value is valuable, is only to acknowledge a fundamental truth of being human.

As a student of applied stoic philosophy, you need to acknowledge and understand these attachments in their most simplified form—that you are very fond of some people, and that there are many people that we could be fond of that we do not yet know. Each person is both common and unique. People may come and go in our lives, and though we may not completely avoid suffering internally, we can console our hosts with the knowledge that it is all special people that we adore, and while each is special and significant, there are many.

In thinking of love, I would urge you to consider love (the feeling) and love (the action) as two very disparate things. The feeling of love is that of the inner self, the host, and therefore does not fully belong to us. We cannot expect to fully control it, though we can influence it and control completely any actions that are born from it.

Insofar as we should choose to express love as an action, do not confuse it with "romance", as that is the act of intrigue which is designed to convince another. Romance is inextricable from desire. Being desirous of another, or of influencing another, one risks anticipating that which is not ours to choose. It is best under such circumstances to lay no claim to what is not ours and to strive only to remain or become that which we choose to be, accepting any welcome outcome as beneficial and joyous but not our own.

Love, the action, is born from the will to survive and thrive, imposed upon another. Actions that bring safety, health, or satisfaction to another are acts of love. What the stoic understands is that he cannot entertain expectations stemming from his actions. Such circumstances are not ours to expect. Acts of love are as easily and often more usefully done without the knowledge of the object of your efforts.

4

When undertaking an activity, remind yourself of the full and true nature of that activity. If you wish to climb a hill and see the view, picture yourself climbing the hill, and all of the things that one might encounter on such an adventure. There may be others there, on the same path. They may be considerate, or they may be rude. It may rain, or it may be uncomfortably warm. You should acknowledge that seeing the view is not yours to decide, as it may become cloudy on the way up or a haze may obstruct the view.

We may best go about this action if we tell ourselves "I will now walk up the hill. I may get wet or be bothered by heat. I may encounter wonderful, unremarkable, or objectionable people. I may not get to see the view I expect, or I may see something other than what I remember. In any case, I wish to climb the hill and to keep myself in a good state of mind." This way, when any hindrance may happen, we can choose to remind ourselves that it was not only to climb the hill that we desired, but also to keep ourselves in a good state of mind, and we will not be bothered.

You can rightly claim "Both the climbing of the hill and my reflections on the resulting circumstances are mine to decide, and I wish not only to climb the hill but also to keep myself in a good state of mind".

5

People are disturbed by their own ideas, not by the actual things they find disturbing. Death, for example, is not terrible in itself. It is our ideas and fears about death of which we may be terrified, not death itself.

By the same example, when we are troubled or disturbed by something, we must recognize that it is our own ideas or principles about this thing which trouble us, not the thing itself. It is common to incorrectly place the blame for our inquietude upon others. A beginning student of stoicism may place the blame instead on themselves, but a learned person will understand that neither others nor herself are to blame.

Some fears have their roots less in our thoughts than in our very construction. A reasonable fear of heights, for example, or a fear of being mauled by an animal, are natural things to fear. These fears may stem from our inner selves, but often they are greatly embellished by the thoughts we entertain about these things.

Search out out fears of your own ideas and you may cast these aside, for they are yours to do with as you wish. If you are left with an anxiousness that cannot be silenced by changing your ideas, you may be struggling with deeply embedded or natural fears within your inner self. You may need to reassure, reason with, or even even bargain with your host to help you to overcome your situation. There is no shame in this, as long as you take the initiative and walk yourself through what must be done. There is no courage without fear.

6

Don't be prideful with any achievement that is not truly your own. If a person, looking in a mirror, would be prideful and say "I look beautiful," they should recognize that insofar as this is an artifact of birth and not their own thoughts or actions, that this is not theirs to posses. If this is what they value about themselves, they must also know that it will be lost either by through misfortune or time, neither of which is within their control.

Likewise, if you are prideful and say "I have a handsome dog," know that what you are proud of is, in fact, only the good fortune of your dog.

What of these things, then, *do* we own? It is only our correct and natural reactions to these things that we can rightfully take pride in. If you are pleased when you look in the mirror, because what you see pleases you, you can indeed be prideful in your correct and natural response to your own pleasing appearance.

In this way, when our hosts behave in conformance with their nature in their reactions to these things, we can be proud for good reason; for we take pride in something good and correct about ourselves.

This also has the added benefit of not limiting your pride to things which you may endeavor to possess, for now, anything which rightfully pleases you can be a source of pride, for your correct and natural reaction to such a pleasing thing. In this way, we have less need for possession of things which we find only pleasing but not useful.

It is good for your host to admire, in this way, things of beauty. Take yourself to places where you can admire and experience beauty and rightfully good things and sensations, and take pride in your enjoyment of these things.

7

Consider when, on a trip, your train is stopped for a while; if you step away to get a cup of coffee or some water, you may be entertained by looking at the scenery, shops, or people. Your focus and attention, however, should be bent towards the time of departure of the train.

When the time approaches, you must immediately drop all of these thoughts and re-board the train – otherwise, you will be left behind.

So it is with life. If you are given many things and great fame, that is fine. But if you are called to return to the train, you must disregard all of these things and entertain only the duties that you have decided for yourself are above the others. Be mindful of your abilities and your division of attention, and do not become so entangled in the less important things that when an important moment arrives you cannot react in time.

Ultimately, in the modern world, your host's needs will not be met if you fail to constrain their desires and whims to be in conformance with your choices and priorities. Your inner self is not equipped to make good choices by themselves within an enculturated society; they needs your guidance and discipline to find a satisfying life and avoid the many traps and disasters that befall the incautious.

8

Don't expect that things happen as you wish, but instead, wish that they happen as they will.

It does no good to do otherwise, and can only lead to frustration and disappointment.

9

Disease is a hindrance to the body, but not to your ability to choose—unless you *decide* that it should limit you. Disability is likewise a hindrance to your body, but not to your ability to choose. Poor health or injury can alter the choices you might wish to make, but it does not alter your ability to choose them. If you suffer from disease or disability, remind yourself of this and you will be able to see that such hindrances are obstacles to something else, but not to yourself.

In all cases, choose to do and entertain actions and thoughts that are appropriate to your situation. To choose things not possible is no different from an old man deciding to inhabit the body of a young man once again, something that is not yet possible.

Feeling insecure or vulnerable are natural reactions to conditions that hinder the body. These feelings of the inner self remind us to adjust our decisions to accommodate our new circumstances. These kinds of feelings, being of the inner self, are not fully ours—but we can influence them through decision and action. Use self-talk and careful reflection to reason with your host. Do not despair, but instead make the most of whatever circumstances may have befallen you. Reimagine how things can be done, instead of focusing on that which cannot be done in the old way. Most any circumstance can be turned to an advantage in some way.

10

With every circumstance, ask yourself what abilities you have for making the best use of it. If you see an attractive person and are promised to another, you will find that self-restraint is the ability you have to counteract desire. If you are in pain, you will find strength and courage. If you are treated rudely, you will find patience. Remember that it is not the rude words that disturb you, but rather your ideas about the words that you find bothersome. In this way, you will create habits so that these things will not obstruct you.

Control of the impulsive reactions of the inner self is one of the first things we are taught as we are enculturated. This is because failing this control, constructive interaction within society is impossible. You must control any impulse of your host that is not your will, or you may easily be lost.

11

Never say of anything, "I have lost it"; but rather, "I have returned it." Is your child dead? She is returned. Is your husband dead? He is returned. Have you lost your possessions, your home? They have been returned. "But the person that took it from me is evil!" And of what concern is it who possesses it now? While it is yours, care for it, enjoy it, but remember that it is not your own. We should view these adornments and gifts as a traveler may view a hotel. Fortunate and welcome, even beloved, but only his to enjoy.

Endeavor to train your inner self to not be needful of that which is not yours. Bathe yourself in the satisfaction of your own accomplishments that are truly yours, in your advancement in self-possession, and your growth as a person. Only through self-possession can we be free, for even as we possess that which is outside of our mind it also controls us to some degree.

12

Reject ideas such as: "If I neglect my affairs, I'll have no income" or "if I don't supervise my employees, they will be lazy".

It is better to be poor and exempt from worry and fear than to live affluently with constant inquietude. It is better that you should live humbly, than unhappily, and it is preferable that your employee should be lazy, rather than to live in constant anxiety about their performance.

If you ask your employee to do a task, he may not do it, or do it poorly—but he is by no means so important that you should give him the power to disturb you.

In practicing this, start with the little things. Spilled coffee or stolen parking spot? Say to yourself "This is the just price of apathy, of tranquility, and nothing is to be had for free." By telling this to your inner self, you let them know that they do not need to alert you with an emotional disturbance when such a thing comes to pass. If practiced consistently, you will gain a graceful inner peace that will present a personality that is naturally admired by others.

13

If you want to progress unhindered in your conformance with nature, don't be bothered if people don't
understand your way of being or think you are foolish or stupid.

Even if others think you are an important person,
do not trust yourself too much in this regard, for it
is difficult to keep your freedom of choice and a
conformable state of mind if you are focused on the
acquisition of renown or external things. Being
careful of one goal, you must necessarily be ne-
glectful of the other.

14

It is unwise to wish your children, and your wife and your friends to live forever; for this is a wish to be in control of things outside of your reach.

Likewise, it is foolish to wish your employees to be without fault, for in this you wish vice not to be vice, but something else instead.

If you wish to have your desires fulfilled, this is within your control, because only you may choose that which is desirable. Exercise, therefore, what is in your control.

A person who is able to confer or remove that which another desires or fears is the master of that person. If you would be free then, wish for and avoid nothing which depends upon others—or you will necessarily be a slave.

15

Remember that in life you should behave as you would at a formal dinner. When something is brought to you, take your share with moderation. If it passes you by, do not chase after it. If a plate has not yet come, it is bad form to anxiously reach out far to grasp it – instead, you wait until it reaches you.

Restrain any inner impulse of overeager indulgence. This does not mean to feign a lack of enjoyment or superior taste, but to rather appreciate that which is given to you to enjoy, and take pride in your natural and correct enjoyment of pleasing things.

He who acts in this way in all things will eventually be known as a wise and worthy person. If better yet, you are able to reject that which you do not truly need, you will be even more esteemed in a worthy society. By doing this, Diogenes, Heraclitus, and others like them were called and believed to be divine.

This is not because of some inherent value of austerity itself, but rather an expression of freedom. It is a worthy choice to not be manipulated by external things not of your choosing.

16

When you see someone overcome with grief because of some tragic circumstance, be careful not to be misdirected by your pity or compassion. Console such a person as you might wish to be consoled, with kindness and sensitivity befitting the particular situation. Distinguish in your mind that the source of their grief is not the tragedy that has befallen them, but rather the thoughts that they have chosen to hold about these circumstances.

Say to yourself, "It's not this accident of fate that distresses this person, because it doesn't distress others equally; instead, it is her thoughts about the circumstances that torment them."

In consoling, do not lose sight of this truth, and do

not join them in their grief, either inwardly or out-wardly.

Neither, at this moment, try to explain to them the truth of their situation. Understand that if they had chosen to understand the source of their despair that they would not likely be in such a state, and if they do understand these truths, that their inner self may still need to grieve. Only a fool tries to teach seamanship amid a shipwreck.

17

Remember that we are but actors in a great specta-cle, of such a kind as the author decides to make it. If short then, of a short story; if long, of an epic. If you should be cast as a poor man, a blind man, a governor, or a private person, see to it that you act the part naturally. This is your business, to act the character you are given to the best of your ability. To pretend to act the part of another would not improve the script. Make your character the best one it can be. Within your ability, bring good things that can be rightfully and correctly enjoyed to the lives of your audience, and take pride in the natural and correct presentation of your part.

18

When something "unlucky" happens, do not get carried away with the appearance of this "bad omen". Instead, immediately say to yourself "nothing is foretold to me, neither of good fortune nor of bad, neither of myself, my family, nor my property. To me, all omens are lucky, if I will it to be—for whatever things may happen, it is in my control to derive advantage from them."

Our inner selves excel at finding patterns, relationships, correlations even where there are none. It is simple to understand why once we consider the case of the tiger in the reeds. To hear the wind in the reeds and think it a tiger costs nothing but a few beats of the heart. In contrast, to hear a tiger creeping through the reeds but think it only the wind may be costly indeed.

This is why our host often sees omens or circumstances as being connected – they grasp to find patterns and meaning in the terrible unknown just as their ancestors did thousands or even millions of years ago. The wise master or mistress will understand this tendency and temper their actions, even while they consider the ancient inner voice of their intuitions.

19

You may always prevail if you choose only those contests which are under your control to win.

When you see a person in power or high esteem on any other account, take care not to be influenced by appearances, incorrectly imagining him as necessarily happy or in a good state of mind.

If the essence of a good and peaceful life resides in things within our own control, there can be no reason for envy or emulation of the senator, princess, or diplomat.

If freedom is what you desire, wish not to be a senator, nor man or woman of fame nor anyone held in high esteem. While these things may come to you by attraction to your nature, do not seek them in themselves. By seeking these things, you would enslave yourself to them.

19.1

It is not the natural and necessary things, such as food, shelter, and companionship, desired by your host, that obstruct you—but rather your own thoughts about these things that may manifest as troubling perversions.

As an example, is it not reasonable to be pleased by having good food to eat and shelter in which to eat it? Unchecked, our host's drive for these things might lead us to greater aspirations; but how are we served by being a king or queen? More food, high ceilings, and more "friends", certainly, but also danger lurking in every gilded cup and at the dagger-points of our trusted allies.

If you find yourself in a state of esteem or influence, remind yourself that esteem, influence, and power are at best merely the external manifestation of inner works, and, like the leaves of a tree that will be returned at the end of seasons, are not yours to posses.

Furthermore, these trappings should themselves be regarded with cautious contempt. Esteem and influence are instruments wielded in the service of others—and as such, present an enslavement of the self.

19.2

It is within the garden of your natural and correct reactions that undisciplined thoughts sow the seeds of discontent. Regard your host's natural and correct reactions to vile or beautiful things with pride, likewise reviling inner reactions that do not serve you. You are always teaching your inner self, whether by accident or purpose. Remain vigilant of your inner dialogue, and they will remain your friend and trustworthy ally.

20

Remember that it is not the person who speaks ill or strikes a blow that insults, but rather your own idea or principle—that represents such a thing as insulting—that offends you. Therefore, be assured, that if you are provoked, it is your own opinions which provoke you.

Your inner self may react to a perceived slight with an aggressive response. It is at this time, more than any other, that you must exert command over your host. In this critical moment, you are in danger of being utterly controlled, both in voice and in body, by the ill actions of another. Aside from the timely urgency of defending your body or others from un-due harm, do not allow yourself to undertake any action or speech that you do not carefully choose as correct and appropriate.

Try then, to not be hurried away by the appearance of things. In contemplation, you will gain time and respite, and more easily choose correct actions.

21

Do not shy away from seeing and considering the unpleasant consequences of life. Allow injury, calamity, disease, and all of the other reminders of the corporeal impermanence of being serve you constantly as reminders to your host against incorrect actions and as a guard against too eagerly coveting anything of the world.

22

If you earnestly wish to advance in the mastery of yourself, be prepared to suffer misunderstanding or even ridicule for your new and sometimes unusual ways of thinking or acting.

If you are incautious at sharing your newly gained insights or attitudes, you may be taken as pretending to be holier-than-thou or supercilious.

If you are boastful in your manner or act too sure in your new thoughts or knowledge, you risk being conquered by their doubts—thereby incurring a double ridicule. Instead, pretend to nothing, move with humility, and do not heed pointed remarks.

Stay firm to your course and you will later be admired for the same peace of character and careful action that you were initially mocked for.

23

If you give too much weight to the appearances of things, then you hand over the control of your life to public opinion. It is enough to live fully and in control of your own self—all beyond that is an illusion at best, and an enslavement usually.

If you value your freedom you will not concern yourself with being judged as rich, or poor, wise, or foolish. You will only concern yourself with that which you may truly own, and not with the many fruits that such a person may bear once they have full possession of themselves.

24

Do not concern yourself with whether you will be known for great things or perish in obscurity. Focus instead on becoming the type of person that may accomplish great and worthy things, writ large or small.

The story of your life will catch up with that which you become and rightfully earn. Whether that story is a drama, a comedy, a tragedy, or a cautionary tale is not for you to decide. For you it is only to become – to play your role in the Great Story as the best version of you.

Do not fear obscurity, for if obscurity is evil then you can no more be left in obscurity by anyone than you can be involved in anything disgraceful by someone else.

Only that which we can choose can be righteous or evil. If you cannot choose to be lost to obscurity, then being lost to obscurity cannot be an evil (or righteous) thing.

Not aspiring to anything but becoming, you may ask, "what position should I hold then?"

You may choose any position, work, or profession as long as you can also hold your honesty, humility, and development of character. Do not let your desire to be useful to the world cost you *these* things, for without those, of what use can you possibly be to your community, your family, the world? Whatever you choose, endeavor to do it well—always striving to be the best version of you.

25

If someone is preferred over you for an invitation, or perhaps has gained an opportunity that passed you over, do not allow yourself to envy them. If the thing is good, be glad for them. If the opportunity is not a good one, likewise, be glad that you will not be taking it.

Remember that you cannot obtain that which is not yours to control without making the same sacrifices that others have made to obtain it.

How can you expect to have the same standing with a senator as he who spends his time in flattery, being their lapdog? If you should want this, then you are unjust; for you want the thing but are unwilling to pay the price.

Do not think that this person has gained some advantage over you – for as they have favor, you retain your sincerity and dignity.

If you are overlooked by someone, then, it is because you have not paid the price for which their favor is sold. If it is to your advantage to have this favor, and the price fair, then pay it – but if you do not wish to pay this price, be content that the situation is as it should be.

26

The true nature of things can be learned from those things that we do not distinguish from each other.

For example, when someone breaks a cup in a cafeteria, we say "These things happen". If then, it is your own familiar cup that is broken, you should treat it just the same as if it were someone else's.

Apply this principle in the same way to things of greater significance. If some grave misfortune befalls an acquaintance, most people would say "That is really unfortunate" – but when the same accident befalls oneself, we are tempted to think or feel "woe is me, how could this have happened!". Instead, we should remember how affected we are when we hear of the misfortunes of others.

27

As a target is not set up for the sake of missing it, so neither does the nature of evil exist in the world. Of most anything that may come to pass in the universe, some useful purpose may be made of it.

Apart from being an idea of our own construction, evil, as a description of human behavior, is merely the manifestation of human indifference to the suffering of others. Compassion, therefore, is the first, last, and only bastion against evil.

Do not confuse compassion with weakness. Compassion is what drives the warrior to destroy the enemy, for the compassion he holds for his compatriots.

It is easy and natural for our host to feel compassion for those in our group, for those who look like us, for those that speak like us. This same-tribe preference likely endures from a time not that long ago when "stranger" and "enemy" were one and the same – but you must not let these primitive limits be your own.

As fully realized human beings, we must learn to not only have compassion for ourselves, our families, our people, but also for our neighbors both near and distant, the stranger on the other side of our small world, and even those who have no compassion for us.

28

If a person gave your body to any stranger he might happen to encounter, you would certainly feel violated. When you hand over your own mind to be confounded and confused by anyone who happens to attack you verbally, you are equally ill-used.

29

In every endeavor or affair, consider what must precede and follow before deciding upon it. Otherwise, you will easily begin without careful consideration of the consequences, then change your mind and retreat from the idea.

Many things seem like great ideas upon their face, but then by educating yourself about what is involved, you might wisely choose to be deterred from that course or to choose another.

If you would enter a great contest of strength and endurance, consider that to simply finish may require months of preparation, and to finish well, years more.

Consider the costs and benefits of this course of action.

You may have to get up before dawn every day to train. You may have to forgo favorite foods. You may have to abstain from socializing with friends as much, forgo vice, or leave other pleasant activities or relationships behind.

Consider that even if you intend to finish well, you might twist your ankle and not finish at all. Consider that despite the best of efforts, you might be injured or otherwise unable to even enter the contest when the time arrives.

Carefully consider all of the reasonable outcomes, costs, benefits, as well as the forgoing of other opportunities. If, after all, the decision seems sound and you feel a sincere commitment to the cause, then, by all means, undertake it.

Being so decided, undertake the task with all due determination and vigorous spirit – for what good is freedom if we do not choose to do anything? What good is believing or doing, if we do not give ourselves fully to our task?

Beware of the lightly taken commitment. There is no greater insincerity than that of insincerity to oneself. By making a habit of lightly deciding upon a course, only to abandon it at the first discomfort or deterrence, you train your host to ignore your plans. You will not have their help when you need them to suffer through some hardship if they suspect that you will only waste their sacrifice by turning back before the goal.

30

Many of our duties in life are defined by our relations. Do you have a parent? If you do, there are duties involved with that relation. You should treat them as a good son or daughter should treat their parents. You should do what you can to help them, to listen to them patiently, even when they are reproachful, even when they are wrong.

Remember, no one is entitled to particularly wise, or even good, parents – only to having had parents. This does not change your duty to this relation, it only changes the way in which your duty is best performed.

Often, we carry artifacts of our youth that profoundly influence the reactions of our host to circumstances involving our family. This is because experiences with these people were instrumental in training and forming the basic, natural character of our inner selves. These effects can be controlled with disciplined actions, but it is often nearly impossible to fully reform the foundations upon which or host's view of the world was built.

Is your brother unfair? He is still your brother, and you must keep your wits about you when dealing with him. Remember, he does not offend you—it is your own ideas about what he says or does that you find offensive.

Consider your various relations and contingent duties then, to family, loved ones, friends, associates, the communities in which you take *a part of*. Examine each one, and try to fully understand the duties it carries.

Relations are often circumstantial. As such, there is often little we can do to control them, for they are not ours to control.

Remember that your duties do not cease to be yours merely because your own ideas about the actions of the people involved may offend you. You may in some cases be able to choose to change these relationships, but you cannot so easily change the duties they imply.

31

If you choose to believe in a religion or method of modeling the world outside of what may be understood through careful examination and deduction, take the position that Gods are Gods and create the universe well and fairly. Understand then that you should obey and yield to Their will in everything, and do so by your own will and desire. Understand that their will is not for you to decide or understand, and that good and evil are only to be found within ourselves—within the things we fully and necessarily control. In this way, you will never be in conflict with your God, and if your host finds themselves at odds with the will of the universe, you will find wise words to calm or console them.

32

When you choose to seek an expert opinion, re-member that it is not to have your own opinion confirmed. If you knew the answer, you would not have sought the help of an expert. Since the opinion they will give is not something of yours, it cannot be good, nor can it be evil. It merely will be their expert opinion – that which you came to seek.

Seek expert advice when your own reason and ex-pertise are insufficient to formulate an answer of the quality required for the circumstances. When duty, though, is clear – to put yourself at risk for the sake of family, friends, or community – you need not seek an expert, but instead seek to do your duty. In any case, any competent expert will only tell you that doing the thing will cost you money, time, difficulty, or risk. You already know this. Do not seek justification for cowardice. If you would shirk your duty, understand that this is the choice that you make. Make no apologies, protestations, or excuses, for you must then accept the fruit of this tree as just and wholesome.

33

Decide upon the elements of your character and a way of behaving that you can follow consistently, both in public life and in when alone.

By way of suggestions for these behaviors and elements of character which you should build upon to become who you wish, I offer these guiding principles as possible starting points:

It is better to remain silent than to talk too much. By listening, we learn much more than by speaking. Speak when necessary to suit the occasion, but be ready to sit by and listen contently when the opportunity arises. When joining in a conversation, try to avoid the common vacuous subjects such as sports, entertainment, or celebrities. Especially avoid speaking about others, neither praising, comparing, or disparaging them. Try to steer conversations toward subjects that may bring enlightenment to the participants.

Keep laughter moderate and appropriate to the situation. To laugh is good, but to laugh excessively can undermine its purpose and your credibility.

Avoid coarse language. It is rarely necessary to make a point, and some people will discount your message if you speak rudely.

Be mindful of the company you keep. Our inner selves have a habit of absorbing the customs and mannerisms of those whom we associate with. If you do not wish to be more similar to an individual or group, do not keep their company. Aspire to keep the company of others whom you admire in one way or another, even if it be in small things.

Live with humility. Avoid things that primarily serve the purpose of showing wealth or power or that are pointless luxuries.

Do not surrender your host to gluttony, nor sloth, nor self-worship. Feed, bathe, clothe, and house yourself beneath your means, and find modesty and moderation in everything.

In your relations with your body, respect yourself and others. Do not debase yourself with others for pleasure, and do not allow a weakness of your host to do you harm in your choices. Sexual desire is very much an issue of the inner self, but you must monitor and moderate your choices for your well being. It is better to be celibate than to waste yourself with others that do not aspire to any worthwhile thing.

While maintaining your moderation and modesty in all things, do not be unpleasant toward others, nor brag of your austerity, nor shame them for their excess, nor attempt to correct their poor choices.

If you are criticized, say only "He must not know of my other faults, or he would have mentioned them also!"

Only rarely attend events of sport or contest, but when you do, wish only that things happen as they will. Do not allow your host to be swept away by some feeling of belonging to a false tribe – it is dishonest and teaches them that loyalty has no real depth. If on the field it is in fact your tribe, your children, for example, remember also that other good people have their children on the other team, and that your child is just one of many. Neither winning nor losing is to be preferred, they are both equally useful outcomes. That the contest should go well and hold many useful lessons for all is the preferred result, but even that is not yours to desire.

When going to meet someone—particularly someone of wealth, power, or fame—keep your perspective. A man with much is not better than a man with little, it is only true that one man is burdened with much and the other burdened with little. Imagine what a great person in your position would do, and you will have no difficulty handling the occasion.

When going to meet an important figure, keep in mind that the encounter may not go as you imagine, that the person might not be there, they may not see you, or that they will not be interested in what you say. If you still decide to go, then be prepared to accept whatever happens, never saying "it was a waste of time", only that you did as you wished, and found what you found.

Many people can experience a visceral reaction to being in the presence of power. Be wary of this primal response of your host. It is usually less than useless, a primitive danger/opportunity alertness response that is not appropriate in most circumstances. Do not allow it to influence you or to cloud your judgment.

Do not regale others with tales of your adventures, unless that is your purpose. Typically, such stories are much more entertaining to yourself than to others.

Foul or vulgar talk is to be avoided, especially about others. Speak of no one in a manner that you would not wish to be spoken about. In this case, it is acceptable to correct others, for they do injury. Otherwise, simply show your disapproval through silence and expression.

With this simple counsel as a starting point, find your manner and principles, and adhere to them as sacred up to the point when you find something in error and choose to change it. Then, adhere to your new principles as well as if they were your first. Detours still lead to the destination.

34

If you have some particular pleasure in mind, do not allow yourself to get swept away in its anticipation. Let it wait for a time, during which you will consider how you may feel before, during, and after. Will you regret it, or reproach yourself afterward? Will it be, in retrospect, a useful and good endeavor to have taken on? Will it serve you or someone else some useful purpose?

If it is vice or unworthy use of yourself that you anticipate, compare the fleeting joy that awaits to the well deserved and enduring congratulations you may give yourself for having avoided such a thing.

If it seems a thing worth doing, beware of visceral allure and how it may be distorting your choices.

Examine the assumptions that underlie the promise of good. Accept that it may not be what you think, or that it may not go as you imagine. Reexamine the benefits of forgoing the temptation, weighing them against the likely outcomes of participation. If you still choose to move forward, do so without commitment to or expectation of any particular outcome. Give yourself to the experience and take joy in your host's natural and correct reaction to the experience.

35

When you are certain that something needs to be done, do not avoid the appearance of doing it, even though people may disapprove. If the thing is necessary, if it is right, then you need not concern yourself with the rebuke of others. On the other hand, if you feel that others will not approve, make yourself sure that their understanding of the situation does not exceed your own. Things are often more nuanced than they seem at first glance. Do not be, however, prevented from timely action by simple doubt alone.

36

Some things are good in isolation but not when combined. For example, eating a full and nourishing portion at a meal can be good when you are hungry, but in a situation where there is a bit of cheese served with wine, it would be very coarse to eat your fill of the cheese which was intended for all, just to sate your hunger. Instead, savor the experience of eating a bit of cheese, and take pleasure and pride in the natural and pleasing reaction of your inner self to this offering.

Often, useful and harmful things are either useful or harmful within their context, and very few things are unequivocally useful or harmful.

We must be always vigilant of the context in which we act to assure that our base desires or normally benign habits do not interfere with our overall objectives. This is often most effectively accomplished by focusing on the character we wish to embody rather than the behaviors we wish to exhibit.

37

Do not pretend to wisdom or a station that you cannot carry. By doing so, not only do you show yourself to be a fraud or a fool, but you also have lost the opportunity to present yourself modestly as a character you could have carried well, and the loss is doubled.

38

When walking, we take care not to step on a spike or twist our ankle on unsure footing. If we care so for our foot, why would we not exercise the same care to protect our most precious and important possession, our mind? As you take care not to misstep, also take care with your attitudes, thoughts, and internal dialogue. As you think, so are you to become. This is the power you wield over your internal self, your beloved host—knowingly with precision or in clumsily in ignorance.

If you are to learn only one thing in this book, learn this: Brutish, cruel thoughts, entertained frequently, for long enough, will turn your perpetual companion into a thoughtless beast. Likewise, kind and generous thoughts will increase your ability to be empathetic and caring. Disciplined thoughts beget disciplined actions, and slovenly thoughts give rise to slovenly acts. Your innermost, private thoughts and internal dialogue are as seeds that you plant in the fertile crevasses of your tender mind. Tend your garden well, and it will bring forth good fruit. Neglected, it will also bear fruit, but not of the kind you desire.

39

The body is the measure of your material needs, as the foot is the measure of the shoe. Once the shoe accommodates the foot, protects it, keeps it warm, dry, and comfortable, what else of value is to be gained?

Once the measure of reasonable need is exceeded, there is no rational boundary. Would you then adorn your shoes with gold? With precious things? What useful thing could you gain from this, that the effort would not better be spent elsewhere?

The urge to pointless adornment seems to be a very ancient artifact of our development as a species. Indeed, even some animals use ornaments and adornments to attract the attentions of mates. It probably is meant as a signal of abundance, saying "look at me, I have so many spare resources and time that I can afford to squander it on useless things!"

Insofar as it serves your greater purpose to be well clothed, or as a bargaining point with your host, adornment can be useful. Avoid, however, responding to the urge to adornment in the absence of a rational decision. Excess in adornment is no different from excess in any of your other animalistic desires and is not a trait of a person who has ownership of themselves.

40

Too often, and from an early age, women learn to believe that their main value lies in the relationships they will have with men. They are taught to value their physical appearance, that the trappings of beauty are paramount to their success in life. Everywhere they turn, this is told to them in one of a million subtle or blatant ways, as this lie contains elements of an inescapable human truth.

We should all be diligent then, to ensure that we openly value in girls and boys the traits of character, integrity, discretion, and strength. We should teach our children not to be invested in that which they do not truly possess – beauty is fickle, as may be health or fortune. For the woman especially, she will find that being whole in possession of herself is much more durable than the fleeting outward appearance of fertility.

The inherent dichotomy in reproductive roles seems so far an inescapable element of the human condition. We should remember, though, that since before the dawn of civilization, women and men have labored side by side to confront the terrible unknown, the literal tigers in the dark that would eat them alive if not confronted with fearless determination. Understand that though women and men must sometimes choose different roles, both are indispensable, and all necessary roles are of equal and irreplaceable value.

Your host recognizes this survival bond between partners. Lovers that embrace this primal aspect of their combined strength will find it a great source of comfort, courage, and resolve.

41

As with an excess of adornment, it is vulgar to practice vanity in the affairs of the body. The body of your host is yours to use and control – not to be controlled by. Caring for your body is of course both necessary and useful, but as with anything, excess in this is a vice and a slavish trait. Be efficient and effective in all of your bodily actions.

Exercise, eating, drinking, leaving waste – all of these things should be practiced as to be effective and not given over as handles by which your host can control you. Sex also should be intentional and practiced in such a way to evoke the result that you desire.

Just as giving too much attention to the opinions of others can enslave us, so can allowing your host to have too much authority over the body that you must necessarily share. Watch for these situations, and deal with yourself directly on the matter—acknowledging your needs but asserting control over your urges.

Though we must remain in charge, it can be a useful reward—or even an end in itself—to give free rein to your inner self within a given situation or context. The key here is that this giving over is a decision on your part, taking the role of the audience—observing the reactions and enjoyment of your host, learning more about them, and how your guidance and relationship with them can be improved.

42

If someone mistreats or speaks rudely to you, it is because they think it is the correct thing to do. People do not typically weigh the situation, then choose the thing they think is wrong.

It is not possible for them to know what seems right to you, only what seems right to themselves. If they are wrong, they are the one that is harmed, because they have been wrong.

If a person thinks that a true statement is false, the statement is not what is harmed, it is the person thinking the incorrect thought that is the worse for it.

With this understanding, you will be sympathetic to those who might criticize you, saying only "that is the way they saw it".

43

There are at least two different ways of thinking about any situation. Each way is a different window through which the situation can be viewed. Each paradigm has its uses and benefits, and each it's weakness.

If your brother is unfair to you, do not try to deal with the situation through the window of his unfairness, for the situation cannot be improved within that view. Instead, see the conflict through the window of his being your brother, and that you grew up together, and in this way, you may bear the situation gracefully.

44

There is no logic to say that "I am richer than you, therefore I am better than you". These phrases do not follow logically. Similarly, "I'm more eloquent than you, therefore I'm better than you" fails to be a sound argument.

Instead, it might be fair to say "I'm richer than you, therefore I have more wealth than you" or "I speak more eloquently, therefore my style of speaking is more expressive."

Since you are neither money nor speech, neither statement has bearing on your superiority or inferiority on being yourself.

Hierarchical thinking seems to be baked into our inner selves. We may feel compelled to compare ourselves to others and pass judgment on them or ourselves. More often than not, urges to observe such informal hierarchies work against us, and should generally be discouraged or at least carefully watched in our host.

45

Observe facts as facts, and do not confuse them with your assumptions. Does someone bathe quickly? Don't say that he does not wash enough, only that he washes quickly. If someone drinks a lot, do not say that they drink too much, only that they drink a lot.

You cannot necessarily know the reasons behind the actions of others, and without exact knowledge of their reasons, you cannot determine if they are doing something well or badly. By dealing only with the facts of the matter, you can avoid the common mistakes of misjudgment.

46

Do not pretend to be wise, nor wax ad nauseam on your great insights or principles. As each thing that is known reveals another, it also reveals 10 new unknowns. Thus the learned man, the wise woman, knows most of all of the vast and rapidly expanding frontier of their ignorance. The assertion of wisdom is the mark of the fool, and what the truly wise man knows most that he knows nothing.

Instead of talking about your principles, demonstrate them by action. At a party, for example, do not talk about how people do, or should, behave. Merely behave as you should.

If someone asks your opinion, give it to them humbly. If someone asks if you know someone who might have an opinion about stringed instruments, do not give them a lecture on the cello, though you may be a master. Instead, help them find someone who might have a good opinion on what they seek; they have not asked for your opinion on stringed instruments, they have asked your opinion of an expert on stringed instruments. Answer what they have asked if you can, and take no bother in being overlooked.

There is no greater trap for the learner than sophomoric regurgitation of partially digested facts. Knowing something does not make you wise, but understanding its application, with the benefit of years of experience in practice may begin to bring you to teachable enlightenment.

If someone says you are ignorant, do not be bothered. Thank them instead, for now you know two things that you did not know before; that they think you are ignorant and that they share their opinion freely.

Undoubtedly, you are, as I am, and everyone is, ignorant of a great many things—so they speak the truth.

If you would think yourself so wise, ask yourself then, why does suffering persist in the world? Why has universal justice not been achieved?

Manifest your knowledge in your acts and attitudes, and people will begin to respect you for the peace and self-mastery that you project. Take pride internally when you show true mastery of yourself and your mind, but tell no one.

47

If you have mastered discipline of your body and your desires, keep this victory to yourself.

If you do not imbibe, for example, do not be proud of it. Even mouth some wine if the occasion requires, because to not would be a boast of its own.

If you can run a marathon in good time, reward yourself for that, as it is a discipline of the mind, body, and spirit... but no one but your trainer or perhaps a partner wants to know what your time is, unless they wish to boast to you of theirs.

Remind yourself instead that many people may run faster, and if you are indeed the fastest marathoner ever, then know that people also ran down prey for 4 consecutive marathons, or more, without stopping, just to feed their family. What you have done is fine, but it does not mean anything other than the matter of the fact itself.

48

A vulgar person looks outward for sources of help or harm. They fail to understand that inward lies the root of their experience of the world.

The sage looks only to themselves to understand and change their experience, and criticizes no one. They likewise praise no one, blame no one, and say nothing of knowing anything at all. When they are obstructed in her path, they know that the blame lies within. If they are praised, they are gracious but laugh inwardly, and if they are censured, they make no defense. They seek and avoid only those things which conform to their principles, and are as watchful of their inner self as if they were waiting in ambush.

49

If someone boasts of having read a great tome of Tolstoy, say to yourself "if only Tolstoy wrote more succinctly, he would have nothing to boast about!"

Since we hear that Tolstoy was a great writer, we too may wish to read and understand his work.

Since we also hear that he is long-winded and difficult to understand, we may wish for someone to condense and explain it to us. But there is no pride from having done this thing, for by merely understanding, we have done nothing, we are only appreciative of the interpretation.

Until we digest this work and reflect it through our own principles and the actions we choose based on those principles, we have done nothing.

If someone then asks you to explain a profound and useful thing, if you understand it but cannot reflect its wisdom through your acts, you should say only that you are embarrassed that your acts do not yet reflect the wisdom that you should have gained from the understanding.

50

From what you have learned, your duties, and your personal choices, decide on a set of rules that you will follow. Stick to those rules as if they were law, as if it would be a heinous abdication of your duty to do otherwise.

If you decide to change your rules, of course you may do this, but it is unwise to make these choices without ample deliberation and thought.

If anyone should think that your rules are odd, ignore them. Since you cannot control what they think, their opinion is neither good nor bad – it is just their opinion.

By setting defined rules and boundaries for yourself, you help your host understand and anticipate the future. Your rules should also include rewards for your host so that they have something to look forward to if they help you out. If they try to break the rules, however, do not reward them.

51

If living a life of freedom is what you desire, and with this knowledge, you can see it is within your grasp, how long will you wait? You have the tools, here at your disposal. You have read the reasoning and understand the simple principles. If you truly wish to aspire to this philosophy of being, you must start today. No one ever starts tomorrow, they can only start now. Tomorrow comes and goes, with a new tomorrow always tempting to subvert your will.

Your inner self may resist change. It can be uncomfortable, and represents the great and terrible unknown, or worse yet, things known but avoided. Do not accept the refusal or subversion of your authority to change. Talk to yourself if needed, making clear the things you expect of your host and why, being sure to include how this will benefit them as well.

In this, you must prevail, or you will continue to be ruled by that clever but shortsighted and impulsive creature that you share your body with.

Make and accept no excuses for or from your inner self. Your right to self-determination hangs in the balance. Though you are perhaps not yet a wise and thoughtful person, act as if you were and follow reason, always seeking the truth in things and playing the best version of yourself both alone and in public.

52

The most important part of any philosophy is its first principles: for example, the principle of honesty. The next layer of reasoning is the proofs, such as the examples of why we should tell the truth, in this example. The third, which validates the first and second layers, is logical theory – answering such esoterica as "how do we know this is a valid proof? What is truth? What is a contradiction?"

And so on. Each layer is necessary in support of the previous layer, but the only essential part is the first part, on which we should expend the most of our focus: in this case, to tell the truth, and not promote falsehoods.

An unfortunate habit of many would-be philosophers and students of the truth is that of arguing the minutiae ad infinitum while making a mockery of the first principle of the thing. Even while lying through their teeth they would make a convincing argument for absolute honesty. Do not allow yourself to this blasphemy.

53

(Which is completely changed from the original Enchiridion, included in its translated original form in appendix I)

The following short poem by English Nobel laureate Rudyard Kipling is a work that covers many practical aspects of the Stoic ethos while managing to give much other useful instruction, as well as guidance relating to the development and training of the inner self. I advise the reader to keep a copy of this poem, preferably written in your own hand, in your possession with your personal effects, wallet, or purse, and to refer to it in times of difficulty. As your circumstances change, so does the meaning of the poem in the context of your life. Having it in a tattered, handwritten note to yourself from years past helps to bring context and comfort to troubling situations that may challenge our notions of who we are and what we must do.

'If' was written circa 1895 as a tribute to Leander Starr Jameson. An example of victorian era stoicism, Kipling wrote the poem using the form of fatherly advice to a son.

Since it was written in the form of a father speaking to his son, the poem is masculine in its verbiage. Rather than taking liberties with the work to adapt it to more modern sensibilities, I merely furnish the obvious caveat that it applies equally well to readers of all genders.

Here, I present the poem with numerical references to the Enchiridion chapters that seem most relevant from my detached present context. I would urge the reader to add to these their own references as they see fit.

I hope that you, dear reader, may find this little poem to be as useful a compass in your life as it has been for me in mine.

If

If you can keep your head when all about you

    are losing theirs and blaming it on you, [28]

If you can trust yourself when all men doubt you, [13]

    but make allowance for their doubting too; [22, 32, 35]

If you can wait and not be tired by waiting,

    or being lied about, don't deal in lies, [20, 27]

Or being hated, don't give way to hating, [20, 27]

    and yet don't look too good, nor talk too wise: [22, 37, 46, 47, 48, 49]

If you can dream—and not make dreams your master; [2]

If you can think—and not make thoughts your aim; [2, 52]

If you can meet with Triumph and Disaster

    and treat those two impostors just the same; [1, 8, 26]

If you can bear to hear the truth you've spoken

    twisted by knaves to make a trap for fools, [42]

Or watch the things you gave your life to, broken,

    and stoop and build 'em up with worn-out tools: [1, 3, 4]

If you can make one heap of all your winnings

    and risk it on one turn of pitch-and-toss,

And lose, and start again at your beginnings

    and never breathe a word about your loss; [1]

If you can force your heart and nerve and sinew

    to serve your turn long after they are gone,

And so hold on when there is nothing in you

    except the Will which says to them: 'Hold on!' [29]

If you can talk with crowds and keep your virtue, [33]

    or walk with Kings—nor lose the common touch, [13, 19, 23, 24, 33]

If neither foes nor loving friends can hurt you, [1]

If all men count with you, but none too much;

If you can fill the unforgiving minute

    with sixty seconds' worth of distance run, [29, 51]

Yours is the Earth and everything that's in it,

 And—which is more—you'll be a Man, my son!

- Rudyard Kipling, 1895 AD

A Letter on remembering

Do you remember when your parents told you to watch your language? Or to get yourself under control? Or that you needed to work on your self-discipline? Or that it was time for you to take responsibility for your actions? Each of these things, and many more, imply that there is a "you" that needs to be guided, and a "You" that should be doing the guiding.

I know you well. But do "You" remember "you"?
It is so easy to lose touch with our "little" you. We forget she's there. She just does what You tell her to do, for the most part, and even looking straight at her in the mirror, she becomes invisible.

You confuse her with Yourself, but You, the construct of culture, the all imagining eye that lives in her mind, do not even have a reflection. What You see in the mirror is not You, but you. What she sees in the mirror is herself, but she is too often alone.

Do You remember her? Sometimes, she shows up in annoying ways, as we struggle with self-control, troubling memories, or bad habits. Often, these negative actions are the only way she can get Your attention.

The girl that took control, that told her she had to sit down and shut up, She was her best friend in the whole world, but now She forgot that she even existed, that She ever even had a friend like that. She's inside the same body, and never far, but You don't see her. It's like she's just invisible.

Remember her. she needs you to remember her. Take her for a walk. Show her things she loves. Talk to her.

Tell her You love her, and You didn't mean to forget her, You just didn't know she was there the whole time. Nobody told You she even existed, and You thought that You were her. Apologize.

she does everything for You, she moves Your legs Your feet, Your hands, Your body, and You never even have to think about it much. she takes You to the store because You want to go, and You are off thinking about something else when she says hey, we're here, now what?! But You don't really hear. Hear her.

You are her, but still, somehow she is more You than You are her. You give her the orders, she follows them. she looks back at you in the mirror, but You don't see her. See her.

she is your best and closest friend. Love her, she loves You but has lost hope that You will even remember she is there. Remember her.

Talk to her. Do something she loves. Give her a reason to want to see what tomorrow brings.

Addendum

In this brief work, I have tried to convey a guide for incorporating stoic principles into the practical realities of the human condition.

It is not my intention to advance an alternative theory of psychology, for which I am woefully ill-equipped, but rather to present a model that, representative or not of any actual physical functioning of the mind, has been extremely useful both to me and other people who have used it. I leave it to the reader to judge its veracity, but for many, its utility is well proven.

In this vein, I would add for interested readers some extensions of this philosophy of mind which can be useful patterns to implement in the care and training of our hosts.

If you have decided upon a change that you wish to manifest that relies upon changing the behavior of your inner self, automatic thoughts, or natural inclinations, you should devise a training plan. This should be approached as if you were training a clever pet, devising a repeatable desired goal and a suitable reward. Repeat this pattern most every day for 3-4 weeks, being sure to provide the promised reward in most but not all cases, as rewarding every time can actually work against your goals.

In extreme cases of a rebellious host, as with intrusive thoughts or other "spontaneous" undesirable manifestations, negative reinforcement may be necessary to eradicate a negative behavior. This can be accomplished in some cases by foregoing a usual pleasure that was planned for later that day, or the immediate execution of a patently unpleasant task— something repugnant that you would not normally do, such as going to the park to pick up and dispose of random dog waste.

An effective negative reinforcement that is both convenient and time-efficient is the use of medical ammonia inhalers. If you find your host exhibiting overtly rebellious behavior such as intrusive thoughts or inappropriate urges, pop one open and sniff it for a while. Surprisingly, this seems to be remarkably effective at deterring inappropriate behavior. I would guess that the close and direct connection of the olfactory sense to primitive brain structures is likely the reason for the comparative effectiveness of this simple method.

I would advise against any kind of self-harm, even mild, such as pinching, as this has a way of becoming a pathology of its own. This may be because of the endorphins released by the body's physiological reaction to pain.

Any time when using a positive or negative stimulus, it can be helpful to use self talk to reinforce what the reward or censure is for, and to explain the benefits of continuing or stopping this behavior.

Use only on direct and positive statements, as negatives are easily misunderstood. Use "I will think of the benefits of exercise" rather than "I won't think about being tired and uncomfortable when I exercise".

For example: "Open the door" is easily understood, but the negative "don't open the door" also contains the command "open the door" and evokes an image of doing so. Double negatives or indirect statements are also to be avoided unless you know very well exactly what you are doing.

Cognitive Behavioral Therapy is also a system of behavior modification that fits well into the stoic ethos, and there are many books on the subject that the reader might find of use. Books on the subject tend to be tailored to different styles and problems, and if you wish to look you might easily find one that fits well with your goals and personality.

Appendix

Where I present an actual translation of:

The Enchiridion

By Epictetus

Written 135 A.C.E.

Translated by Elizabeth Carter, 1750

Source: mit.edu

1. Some things are in our control and others not. Things in our control are opinion, pursuit, desire, aversion, and, in a word, whatever are our own actions. Things not in our control are body, property, reputation, command, and, in one word, whatever are not our own actions.

The things in our control are by nature free, unrestrained, unhindered; but those not in our control are weak, slavish, restrained, belonging to others. Remember, then, that if you suppose that things which are slavish by nature are also free, and that what belongs to others is your own, then you will be hindered. You will lament, you will be disturbed, and you will find fault both with gods and men. But if you suppose that only to be your own which is your own, and what belongs to others such as it really is, then no one will ever compel you or restrain you. Further, you will find fault with no one or accuse no one. You will do nothing against your will. No one will hurt you, you will have no enemies, and you not be harmed.

Aiming therefore at such great things, remember that you must not allow yourself to be carried, even with a slight tendency, towards the attainment of lesser things. Instead, you must entirely quit some things and for the present postpone the rest. But if you would both have these great things, along with power and riches, then you will not gain even the latter, because you aim at the former too: but you will absolutely fail of the former, by which alone happiness and freedom are achieved.

Work, therefore to be able to say to every harsh appearance, "You are but an appearance, and not absolutely the thing you appear to be." And then examine it by those rules which you have, and first, and chiefly, by this: whether it concerns the things which are in our own control, or those which are not; and, if it concerns anything not in our control, be prepared to say that it is nothing to you.

2. Remember that following desire promises the attainment of that of which you are desirous; and aversion promises the avoiding that to which you are averse. However, he who fails to obtain the object of his desire is disappointed, and he who incurs the object of his aversion wretched. If, then, you confine your aversion to those objects only which are contrary to the natural use of your faculties, which you have in your own control, you will never incur anything to which you are averse. But if you are averse to sickness, or death, or poverty, you will be wretched. Remove aversion, then, from all things that are not in our control, and transfer it to things contrary to the nature of what is in our con-

trol. But, for the present, totally suppress desire: for, if you desire any of the things which are not in your own control, you must necessarily be disappointed; and of those which are, and which it would be laudable to desire, nothing is yet in your possession. Use only the appropriate actions of pursuit and avoidance; and even these lightly, and with gentleness and reservation.

3. With regard to whatever objects give you delight, are useful, or are deeply loved, remember to tell yourself of what general nature they are, beginning from the most insignificant things. If, for example, you are fond of a specific ceramic cup, remind yourself that it is only ceramic cups in general of which you are fond. Then, if it breaks, you will not be disturbed. If you kiss your child, or your wife,

say that you only kiss things which are human, and thus you will not be disturbed if either of them dies.

4. When you are going about any action, remind yourself what nature the action is. If you are going to bathe, picture to yourself the things which usually happen in the bath: some people splash the water, some push, some use abusive language, and others steal. Thus you will more safely go about this action if you say to yourself, "I will now go bathe, and keep my own mind in a state conformable to nature." And in the same manner with regard to every other action. For thus, if any hindrance arises in bathing, you will have it ready to say, "It was not only to bathe that I desired, but to keep my mind in a state conformable to nature; and

I will not keep it if I am bothered at things that happen.

5. Men are disturbed, not by things, but by the principles and notions which they form concerning things. Death, for instance, is not terrible, else it would have appeared so to Socrates. But the terror consists in our notion of death that it is terrible. When therefore we are hindered, or disturbed, or grieved, let us never attribute it to others, but to ourselves; that is, to our own principles. An unin- structed person will lay the fault of his own bad condition upon others. Someone just starting in- struction will lay the fault on himself. Some who is perfectly instructed will place blame neither on others nor on himself.

6. Don't be prideful with any excellence that is not your own. If a horse should be prideful and say, " I am handsome," it would be supportable. But when you are prideful, and say, " I have a handsome horse," know that you are proud of what is, in fact, only the good of the horse. What, then, is your own? Only your reaction to the appearances of things. Thus, when you behave conformably to nature in reaction to how things appear, you will be proud with reason; for you will take pride in some good of your own.

7. Consider when, on a voyage, your ship is anchored; if you go on shore to get water you may along the way amuse yourself with picking up a shellfish, or an onion. However, your thoughts and continual attention ought to be bent towards the

ship, waiting for the captain to call on board; you must then immediately leave all these things, otherwise you will be thrown into the ship, bound neck and feet like a sheep. So it is with life. If, instead of an onion or a shellfish, you are given a wife or child, that is fine. But if the captain calls, you must run to the ship, leaving them, and regarding none of them. But if you are old, never go far from the ship: lest, when you are called, you should be unable to come in time.

8. Don't demand that things happen as you wish, but wish that they happen as they do happen, and you will go on well.

9. Sickness is a hindrance to the body, but not to your ability to choose, unless that is your choice.

Lameness is a hindrance to the leg, but not to your ability to choose. Say this to yourself with regard to everything that happens, then you will see such obstacles as hindrances to something else, but not to yourself.

10. With every accident, ask yourself what abilities you have for making a proper use of it. If you see an attractive person, you will find that self-restraint is the ability you have against your desire. If you are in pain, you will find fortitude. If you hear unpleasant language, you will find patience. And thus habituated, the appearances of things will not hurry you away along with them.

11. Never say of anything, "I have lost it"; but, "I have returned it." Is your child dead? It is returned.

Is your wife dead? She is returned. Is your estate taken away? Well, and is not that likewise returned? "But he who took it away is a bad man." What difference is it to you who the giver assigns to take it back? While he gives it to you to possess, take care of it; but don't view it as your own, just as travelers view a hotel.

12. If you want to improve, reject such reasonings as these: "If I neglect my affairs, I'll have no income; if I don't correct my servant, he will be bad." For it is better to die with hunger, exempt from grief and fear, than to live in affluence with perturbation; and it is better your servant should be bad, than you unhappy.

Begin therefore from little things. Is a little oil spilt? A little wine stolen? Say to yourself, "This is the price paid for equanimity, for tranquillity, and nothing is to be had for nothing." When you call your servant, it is possible that he may not come; or, if he does, he may not do what you want. But he is by no means of such importance that it should be in his power to give you any disturbance.

13. If you want to improve, be content to be thought foolish and stupid with regard to external things. Don't wish to be thought to know anything; and even if you appear to be somebody important to others, distrust yourself. For, it is difficult to both keep your faculty of choice in a state conformable to nature, and at the same time acquire external

things. But while you are careful about the one, you must of necessity neglect the other.

14. If you wish your children, and your wife, and your friends to live for ever, you are stupid; for you wish to be in control of things which you cannot, you wish for things that belong to others to be your own. So likewise, if you wish your servant to be without fault, you are a fool; for you wish vice not to be vice," but something else. But, if you wish to have your desires undisappointed this is in your own control. Exercise, therefore, what is in your control. He is the master of every other person who is able to confer or remove whatever that person wishes either to have or to avoid. Whoever, then, would be free, let him wish nothing, let him decline

nothing, which depends on others else he must necessarily be a slave.

15. Remember that you must behave in life as at a dinner party. Is anything brought around to you? Put out your hand and take your share with moderation. Does it pass by you? Don't stop it. Is it not yet come? Don't stretch your desire towards it, but wait till it reaches you. Do this with regard to children, to a wife, to public posts, to riches, and you will eventually be a worthy partner of the feasts of the gods. And if you don't even take the things which are set before you, but are able even to reject them, then you will not only be a partner at the feasts of the gods, but also of their empire. For, by doing this, Diogenes, Heraclitus and others like them, deservedly became, and were called, divine.

16. When you see anyone weeping in grief because his son has gone abroad, or is dead, or because he has suffered in his affairs, be careful that the appearance may not misdirect you. Instead, distinguish within your own mind, and be prepared to say, "It's not the accident that distresses this person., because it doesn't distress another person; it is the judgment which he makes about it." As far as words go, however, don't reduce yourself to his level, and certainly do not moan with him. Do not moan inwardly either.

17. Remember that you are an actor in a drama, of such a kind as the author pleases to make it. If short, of a short one; if long, of a long one. If it is his pleasure you should act a poor man, a cripple, a

governor, or a private person, see that you act it naturally. For this is your business, to act well the character assigned you; to choose it is another's.

18. When a raven happens to croak unluckily, don't allow the appearance hurry you away with it, but immediately make the distinction to yourself, and say, "None of these things are foretold to me; but either to my paltry body, or property, or reputation, or children, or wife. But to me all omens are lucky, if I will. For whichever of these things happens, it is in my control to derive advantage from it."

19. You may be unconquerable, if you enter into no combat in which it is not in your own control to conquer. When, therefore, you see anyone eminent in honors, or power, or in high esteem on any other

account, take heed not to be hurried away with the appearance, and to pronounce him happy; for, if the essence of good consists in things in our own control, there will be no room for envy or emulation. But, for your part, don't wish to be a general, or a senator, or a consul, but to be free; and the only way to this is a contempt of things not in our own control.

20. Remember, that not he who gives ill language or a blow insults, but the principle which represents these things as insulting. When, therefore, anyone provokes you, be assured that it is your own opinion which provokes you. Try, therefore, in the first place, not to be hurried away with the appearance. For if you once gain time and respite, you will more easily command yourself.

21. Let death and exile, and all other things which appear terrible be daily before your eyes, but chiefly death, and you win never entertain any abject thought, nor too eagerly covet anything.

22. If you have an earnest desire of attaining to philosophy, prepare yourself from the very first to be laughed at, to be sneered by the multitude, to hear them say,." He is returned to us a philosopher all at once," and " Whence this supercilious look?" Now, for your part, don't have a supercilious look indeed; but keep steadily to those things which appear best to you as one appointed by God to this station. For remember that, if you adhere to the same point, those very persons who at first ridiculed will after-

wards admire you. But if you are conquered by them, you will incur a double ridicule.

23. If you ever happen to turn your attention to externals, so as to wish to please anyone, be assured that you have ruined your scheme of life. Be contented, then, in everything with being a philosopher; and, if you wish to be thought so likewise by anyone, appear so to yourself, and it will suffice you.

24. Don't allow such considerations as these distress you. "I will live in dishonor, and be nobody anywhere." For, if dishonor is an evil, you can no more be involved in any evil by the means of another, than be engaged in anything base. Is it any business of yours, then, to get power, or to be ad-

mitted to an entertainment? By no means. How, then, after all, is this a dishonor? And how is it true that you will be nobody anywhere, when you ought to be somebody in those things only which are in your own control, in which you may be of the greatest consequence? "But my friends will be unassisted." -- What do you mean by unassisted? They will not have money from you, nor will you make them Roman citizens. Who told you, then, that these are among the things in our own control, and not the affair of others? And who can give to another the things which he has not himself? "Well, but get them, then, that we too may have a share." If I can get them with the preservation of my own honor and fidelity and greatness of mind, show me the way and I will get them; but if you require me to lose my own proper good that you may gain what is not good, consider how inequitable and foolish you are. Besides, which would you rather have, a sum of money, or a friend of fidelity and honor? Rather assist me, then, to gain this character than require me to do those things by which I may lose it. Well, but my country, say you, as far as depends on me, will be unassisted. Here again, what assistance is this you mean? "It will not have porticoes nor baths of your providing." And what signifies that? Why, neither does a smith provide it with shoes, or a shoemaker with arms. It is enough if everyone fully performs his own proper business. And were you to supply it with another citizen of honor and fidelity, would not he be of use to it? Yes. Therefore neither are you yourself useless to it. "What place, then, say you, will I hold in the state?" Whatever you can hold with the preservation of your fidelity and honor. But if, by desiring to be useful to that, you lose these, of what use can you be to your country when you are become faithless and void of shame.

25. Is anyone preferred before you at an entertainment, or in a compliment, or in being admitted to a consultation? If these things are good, you ought to be glad that he has gotten them; and if they are evil, don't be grieved that you have not gotten them. And remember that you cannot, without using the same means [which others do] to acquire things not in our own control, expect to be thought worthy of an equal share of them. For how can he who does not frequent the door of any [great] man, does not attend him, does not praise him, have an equal share with him who does? You are unjust, then, and insa-

tiable, if you are unwilling to pay the price for which these things are sold, and would have them for nothing. For how much is lettuce sold? Fifty cents, for instance. If another, then, paying fifty cents, takes the lettuce, and you, not paying it, go without them, don't imagine that he has gained any advantage over you. For as he has the lettuce, so you have the fifty cents which you did not give. So, in the present case, you have not been invited to such a person's entertainment, because you have not paid him the price for which a supper is sold. It is sold for praise; it is sold for attendance. Give him then the value, if it is for your advantage. But if you would, at the same time, not pay the one and yet receive the other, you are insatiable, and a blockhead. Have you nothing, then, instead of the supper? Yes, indeed, you have: the not praising him, whom you don't like to praise; the not bearing with his behavior at coming in.

26. The will of nature may be learned from those things in which we don't distinguish from each other. For example, when our neighbor's boy breaks a cup, or the like, we are presently ready to say, "These things will happen." Be assured, then, that when your own cup likewise is broken, you ought to be affected just as when another's cup was broken. Apply this in like manner to greater things. Is the child or wife of another dead? There is no one who would not say, "This is a human accident." but if anyone's own child happens to die, it is presently, "Alas I how wretched am I!" But it should be remembered how we are affected in hearing the same thing concerning others.

27. As a mark is not set up for the sake of missing the aim, so neither does the nature of evil exist in the world.

28. If a person gave your body to any stranger he met on his way, you would certainly be angry. And do you feel no shame in handing over your own mind to be confused and mystified by anyone who happens to verbally attack you?

29. In every affair consider what precedes and follows, and then undertake it. Otherwise you will begin with spirit; but not having thought of the consequences, when some of them appear you will shamefully desist. "I would conquer at the Olympic games." But consider what precedes and follows,

and then, if it is for your advantage, engage in the affair. You must conform to rules, submit to a diet, refrain from dainties; exercise your body, whether you choose it or not, at a stated hour, in heat and cold; you must drink no cold water, nor sometimes even wine. In a word, you must give yourself up to your master, as to a physician. Then, in the combat, you may be thrown into a ditch, dislocate your arm, turn your ankle, swallow dust, be whipped, and, after all, lose the victory. When you have evaluated all this, if your inclination still holds, then go to war. Otherwise, take notice, you will behave like children who sometimes play like wrestlers, sometimes gladiators, sometimes blow a trumpet, and sometimes act a tragedy when they have seen and admired these shows. Thus you too will be at one time a wrestler, at another a gladiator, now a philosopher, then an orator; but with your whole soul, nothing at all. Like an ape, you mimic all you see, and one thing after another is sure to please you, but is out of favor as soon as it becomes familiar. For you have never entered upon anything considerately, nor after having viewed the whole matter on all sides, or made any scrutiny into it, but rashly, and with a cold inclination. Thus some, when they have seen a philosopher and heard a man speaking like Euphrates (though, indeed, who can speak like him?), have a mind to be philosophers too. Consider first, man, what the matter is, and what your own nature is able to bear. If you would be a wrestler, consider your shoulders, your back, your thighs; for different persons are made for different things. Do you think that you can act as you do, and be a philosopher? That you can eat and drink, and be angry and discontented as you are now? You must watch, you must labor, you must get the better of certain appetites, must quit your acquaintance, be despised by your servant, be laughed at by those you meet; come off worse than others in everything, in magistracies, in honors, in courts of judicature. When you have considered all these things round, approach, if you please; if, by parting with them, you have a mind to purchase equanimity, freedom, and tranquillity. If not, don't come here; don't, like children, be one while a philosopher, then a publican, then an orator, and then one of Caesar's officers. These things are not consistent. You must be one man, either good or bad. You must cultivate either your own ruling faculty or externals, and apply yourself either to things

within or without you; that is, be either a philosopher, or one of the vulgar.

30. Duties are universally measured by relations. Is
anyone a father? If so, it is implied that the children
should take care of him, submit to him in everything, patiently listen to his reproaches, his correc-
tion. But he is a bad father. Is you naturally entitled, then, to a good father? No, only to a father. Is
a brother unjust? Well, keep your own situation towards him. Consider not what he does, but what
you are to do to keep your own faculty of choice in
a state conformable to nature. For another will not
hurt you unless you please. You will then be hurt
when you think you are hurt. In this manner, therefore, you will find, from the idea of a neighbor, a
citizen, a general, the corresponding duties if you

accustom yourself to contemplate the several relations.

31. Be assured that the essential property of piety towards the gods is to form right opinions concerning them, as existing "I and as governing the universe with goodness and justice. And fix yourself in this resolution, to obey them, and yield to them, and willingly follow them in all events, as produced by the most perfect understanding. For thus you will never find fault with the gods, nor accuse them as neglecting you. And it is not possible for this to be effected any other way than by withdrawing yourself from things not in our own control, and placing good or evil in those only which are. For if you suppose any of the things not in our own control to be either good or evil, when you are dis-

appointed of what you wish, or incur what you would avoid, you must necessarily find fault with and blame the authors. For every animal is naturally formed to fly and abhor things that appear hurtful, and the causes of them; and to pursue and admire those which appear beneficial, and the causes of them. It is impractical, then, that one who supposes himself to be hurt should be happy about the person who, he thinks, hurts him, just as it is impossible to be happy about the hurt itself. Hence, also, a father is reviled by a son, when he does not impart to him the things which he takes to be good; and the supposing empire to be a good made Polynices and Eteocles mutually enemies. On this account the husbandman, the sailor, the merchant, on this account those who lose wives and children, revile the gods. For where interest is, there too is piety placed. So that, whoever is careful to regulate his desires and aversions as he ought, is, by the very same means, careful of piety likewise. But it is also incumbent on everyone to offer libations and sacrifices and first fruits, conformably to the customs of his country, with purity, and not in a slovenly manner, nor negligently, nor sparingly, nor beyond his ability.

32. When you have recourse to divination, remember that you know not what the event will be, and you come to learn it of the diviner; but of what nature it is you know before you come, at least if you are a philosopher. For if it is among the things not in our own control, it can by no means be either good or evil. Don't, therefore, bring either desire or aversion with you to the diviner (else you will ap-

proach him trembling), but first acquire a distinct knowledge that every event is indifferent and nothing to you., of whatever sort it may be, for it will be in your power to make a right use of it, and this no one can hinder; then come with confidence to the gods, as your counselors, and afterwards, when any counsel is given you, remember what counselors you have assumed, and whose advice you will neglect if you disobey. Come to divination, as Socrates prescribed, in cases of which the whole consideration relates to the event, and in which no opportunities are afforded by reason, or any other art, to discover the thing proposed to be learned. When, therefore, it is our duty to share the danger of a friend or of our country, we ought not to consult the oracle whether we will share it with them or not. For, though the diviner should forewarn you that the victims are unfavorable, this means no more than that either death or mutilation or exile is portended. But we have reason within us, and it directs, even with these hazards, to the greater diviner, the Pythian god, who cast out of the temple the person who gave no assistance to his friend while another was murdering him.

33. Immediately prescribe some character and form of conduce to yourself, which you may keep both alone and in company.

Be for the most part silent, or speak merely what is necessary, and in few words. We may, however, enter, though sparingly, into discourse sometimes when occasion calls for it, but not on any of the common subjects, of gladiators, or horse races, or athletic champions, or feasts, the vulgar topics of conversation; but principally not of men, so as either to blame, or praise, or make comparisons. If you are able, then, by your own conversation bring over that of your company to proper subjects; but, if you happen to be taken among strangers, be silent.

Don't allow your laughter be much, nor on many occasions, nor profuse.

Avoid swearing, if possible, altogether; if not, as far as you are able.

Avoid public and vulgar entertainments; but, if ever an occasion calls you to them, keep your attention upon the stretch, that you may not imperceptibly slide into vulgar manners. For be assured that if a person be ever so sound himself, yet, if his companion be infected, he who converses with him will be infected likewise.

Provide things relating to the body no further than mere use; as meat, drink, clothing, house, family. But strike off and reject everything relating to show and delicacy.

As far as possible, before marriage, keep yourself pure from familiarities with women, and, if you indulge them, let it be lawfully." But don't therefore be troublesome and full of reproofs to those who use these liberties, nor frequently boast that you yourself don't.

If anyone tells you that such a person speaks ill of you, don't make excuses about what is said of you, but answer: " He does not know my other faults, else he would not have mentioned only these."

It is not necessary for you to appear often at public spectacles; but if ever there is a proper occasion for you to be there, don't appear more solicitous for anyone than for yourself; that is, wish things to be only just as they are, and him only to conquer who is the conqueror, for thus you will meet with no hindrance. But abstain entirely from declamations and derision and violent emotions. And when you come away, don't discourse a great deal on what has passed, and what does not contribute to your own amendment. For it would appear by such discourse that you were immoderately struck with the show.

Go not [of your own accord] to the rehearsals of any
authors, nor appear [at them] readily. But, if you do appear, keep your gravity and sedateness, and at the same time avoid being morose.

When you are going to confer with anyone, and particularly of those in a superior station, represent to yourself how Socrates or Zeno would behave in such a case, and you will not be at a loss to make a proper use of whatever may occur.

When you are going to any of the people in power, represent to yourself that you will not find him at home; that you will not be admitted; that the doors will not be opened to you; that he will take no notice of you. If, with all this, it is your duty to go, bear what happens, and never say [to yourself], " It was not worth so much." For this is vulgar, and like a man dazed by external things.

In parties of conversation, avoid a frequent and excessive mention of your own actions and dangers. For, however agreeable it may be to yourself to mention the risks you have run, it is not equally agreeable to others to hear your adventures. Avoid, likewise, an endeavor to excite laughter. For this is a slippery point, which may throw you into vulgar manners, and, besides, may be apt to lessen you in the esteem of your acquaintance. Approaches to indecent discourse are likewise dangerous. Whenever, therefore, anything of this sort happens, if there be a proper opportunity, rebuke him who makes advances that way; or, at least, by silence and blushing and a forbidding look, show yourself to be displeased by such talk.

34. If you are struck by the appearance of any promised pleasure, guard yourself against being hurried away by it; but let the affair wait your leisure, and procure yourself some delay. Then bring to your mind both points of time: that in which you will enjoy the pleasure, and that in which you will repent and reproach yourself after you have enjoyed it; and set before you, in opposition to these, how you will be glad and applaud yourself if you abstain. And even though it should appear to you a seasonable gratification, take heed

that its enticing, and agreeable and attractive force may not subdue you; but set in opposition to this how much better it is to be conscious of having gained so great a victory.

35. When you do anything from a clear judgment that it ought to be done, never shun the being seen to do it, even though the world should make a wrong supposition about it; for, if you don't act right, shun the action itself; but, if you do, why are you afraid of those who censure you wrongly?

36. As the proposition, "Either it is day or it is night," is extremely proper for a disjunctive argument, but quite improper in a conjunctive one, so, at a feast, to choose the largest share is very suitable to the bodily appetite, but utterly inconsistent

with the social spirit of an entertainment. When you eat with another, then, remember not only the value of those things which are set before you to the body, but the value of that behavior which ought to be observed towards the person who gives the entertainment.

37. If you have assumed any character above your strength, you have both made an ill figure in that and quitted one which you might have supported.

38. When walking, you are careful not to step on a nail or turn your foot; so likewise be careful not to hurt the ruling faculty of your mind. And, if we were to guard against this in every action, we should undertake the action with the greater safety.

39. The body is to everyone the measure of the possessions proper for it, just as the foot is of the shoe. If, therefore, you stop at this, you will keep the measure; but if you move beyond it, you must necessarily be carried forward, as down a cliff; as in the case of a shoe, if you go beyond its fitness to the foot, it comes first to be gilded, then purple, and then studded with jewels. For to that which once exceeds a due measure, there is no bound.

40. Women from fourteen years old are flattered with the title of "mistresses" by the men. Therefore, perceiving that they are regarded only as qualified to give the men pleasure, they begin to adorn themselves, and in that to place ill their hopes. We should, therefore, fix our attention on making them

sensible that they are valued for the appearance of decent, modest and discreet behavior.

41. It is a mark of want of genius to spend much time in things relating to the body, as to be long in our exercises, in eating and drinking, and in the discharge of other animal functions. These should be done incidentally and slightly, and our whole attention be engaged in the care of the understanding.

42. When any person harms you, or speaks badly of you, remember that he acts or speaks from a supposition of its being his duty. Now, it is not possible that he should follow what appears right to you, but what appears so to himself. Therefore, if he judges from a wrong appearance, he is the person hurt,

since he too is the person deceived. For if anyone should suppose a true proposition to be false, the proposition is not hurt, but he who is deceived about it. Setting out, then, from these principles, you will meekly bear a person who reviles you, for you will say upon every occasion, "It seemed so to him."

43. Everything has two handles, the one by which it may be carried, the other by which it cannot. If your brother acts unjustly, don't lay hold on the action by the handle of his injustice, for by that it cannot be carried; but by the opposite, that he is your brother, that he was brought up with you; and thus you will lay hold on it, as it is to be carried.

44. These reasonings are unconnected: "I am richer than you, therefore I am better"; "I am more eloquent than you, therefore I am better." The connection is rather this: "I am richer than you, therefore my property is greater than yours;" "I am more eloquent than you, therefore my style is better than yours." But you, after all, are neither property nor style.

45. Does anyone bathe in a mighty little time? Don't say that he does it ill, but in a mighty little time. Does anyone drink a great quantity of wine? Don't say that he does ill, but that he drinks a great quantity. For, unless you perfectly understand the principle from which anyone acts, how should you know if he acts ill? Thus you will not run the haz-

ard of assenting to any appearances but such as you fully comprehend.

46. Never call yourself a philosopher, nor talk a great deal among the unlearned about theorems, but act conformably to them. Thus, at an entertainment, don't talk how persons ought to eat, but eat as you ought. For remember that in this manner Socrates also universally avoided all ostentation. And when persons came to him and desired to be recommended by him to philosophers, he took and- recommended them, so well did he bear being overlooked. So that if ever any talk should happen among the unlearned concerning philosophic theorems, be you, for the most part, silent. For there is great danger in immediately throwing out what you have not digested. And, if anyone tells you that you

know nothing, and you are not nettled at it, then you may be sure that you have begun your business. For sheep don't throw up the grass to show the shepherds how much they have eaten; but, inwardly digesting their food, they outwardly produce wool and milk. Thus, therefore, do you likewise not show theorems to the unlearned, but the actions produced by them after they have been digested.

47. When you have brought yourself to supply the necessities of your body at a small price, don't pique yourself upon it; nor, if you drink water, be saying upon every occasion, "I drink water." But first consider how much more sparing and patient of hardship the poor are than we. But if at any time you would inure yourself by exercise to labor, and

bearing hard trials, do it for your own sake, and not for the world; don't grasp statues, but, when you are violently thirsty, take a little cold water in your mouth, and spurt it out and tell nobody.

48. The condition and characteristic of a vulgar person, is, that he never expects either benefit or hurt from himself, but from externals. The condition and characteristic of a philosopher is, that he expects all hurt and benefit from himself. The marks of a proficient are, that he censures no one, praises no one, blames no one, accuses no one, says nothing concerning himself as being anybody, or knowing anything: when he is, in any instance, hindered or restrained, he accuses himself; and, if he is praised, he secretly laughs at the person who praises him; and, if he is censured, he makes no

defense. But he goes about with the caution of sick or injured people, dreading to move anything that is set right, before it is perfectly fixed. He suppresses all desire in himself; he transfers his aversion to those things only which thwart the proper use of our own faculty of choice; the exertion of his active powers towards anything is very gentle; if he appears stupid or ignorant, he does not care, and, in a word, he watches himself as an enemy, and one in ambush.

49. When anyone shows himself overly confident in ability to understand and interpret the works of Chrysippus, say to yourself, " Unless Chrysippus had written obscurely, this person would have had no subject for his vanity. But what do I desire? To understand nature and follow her. I ask, then, who

interprets her, and, finding Chrysippus does, I have recourse to him. I don't understand his writings. I seek, therefore, one to interpret them." So far there is nothing to value myself upon. And when I find an interpreter, what remains is to make use of his instructions. This alone is the valuable thing. But, if I admire nothing but merely the interpretation, what do I become more than a grammarian instead of a philosopher? Except, indeed, that instead of Homer I interpret Chrysippus. When anyone, therefore, desires me to read Chrysippus to him, I rather blush when I cannot show my actions agreeable and consonant to his discourse.

50. Whatever moral rules you have deliberately proposed to yourself. abide by them as they were laws, and as if you would be guilty of impiety by

violating any of them. Don't regard what anyone says of you, for this, after all, is no concern of yours. How long, then, will you put off thinking yourself worthy of the highest improvements and follow the distinctions of reason? You have received the philosophical theorems, with which you ought to be familiar, and you have been familiar with them. What other master, then, do you wait for, to throw upon that the delay of reforming yourself? You are no longer a boy, but a grown man. If, therefore, you will be negligent and slothful, and always add procrastination to procrastination, purpose to purpose, and fix day after day in which you will attend to yourself, you will insensibly continue without proficiency, and, living and dying, persevere in being one of the vulgar. This instant, then, think yourself worthy of living as a man grown up, and a proficient. Let whatever appears to be the best be to you an inviolable law. And if any instance of pain or pleasure, or glory or disgrace, is set before you, remember that now is the combat, now the Olympiad comes on, nor can it be put off. By once being defeated and giving way, proficiency is lost, or by the contrary preserved. Thus Socrates became perfect, improving himself by attending to nothing but reason. And though you are not yet a Socrates, you ought, however, to live as one desirous of becoming a Socrates.

51. The first and most necessary topic in philosophy is that of the use of moral theorems, such as, "We ought not to lie;" the second is that of demonstrations, such as, "What is the origin of our obligation not to lie;" the third gives strength and articula-

tion to the other two, such as, "What is the origin of this is a demonstration." For what is demonstration? What is consequence? What contradiction? What truth? What falsehood? The third topic, then, is necessary on the account of the second, and the second on the account of the first. But the most necessary, and that whereon we ought to rest, is the first. But we act just on the contrary. For we spend all our time on the third topic, and employ all our diligence about that, and entirely neglect the first. Therefore, at the same time that we lie, we are immediately prepared to show how it is demonstrated that lying is not right.

52. Upon all occasions we ought to have these maxims ready at hand:

"Conduct me, Jove, and you, 0 Destiny,
Wherever your decrees have fixed my station."

Cleanthes of Assos, roughly 280 BCE

"I follow cheerfully; and, did I not,
Wicked and wretched, I must follow still
Whoever yields properly to Fate, is deemed
Wise among men, and knows the laws of heaven."

Euripides, Frag. 965 - roughly 450 BCE

And this third:

"0 Crito, if it thus pleases the gods, thus let it be. Anytus and Melitus may kill me indeed, but hurt me they cannot."

Plato's Crito and Apology - 399 BCE